THE GREEN PARAKEET

THE GREEN PARAKEET

Desmond Graham

FlambardPress

First published in Great Britain in 2009 by Flambard Press
16 Black Swan Court, 69 Westgate Road, Newcastle upon Tyne NE1 1SG
www.flambardpress.co.uk

Typeset by BookType
Cover Design by Gainford Design Associates
Cover image from an embroidery by Trude Schwab © 2009

Printed in Great Britain by Cpod, Trowbridge, Wiltshire

A CIP catalogue record for this book is available from the British Library.

ISBN: 9781906601041

Flambard Press wishes to thank Arts Council England
for its financial support.

Flambard Press is a member of Inpress.

Mixed Sources
Product group from well-managed
forests and other controlled source
www.fsc.org Cert no. TT-COC-2082
© 1996 Forest Stewardship Council
FSC

Contents

Poems for Alan

Postcards from Germany

'Poems for Alan'
are dedicated to the memory of my brother
Alan Graham (1936–2007)
whose love of poetry
shared with me from childhood
lies behind it all

'Postcards from Germany'
are dedicated
to my German friends

Poems for Alan

Peasmarsh

How we laughed
rolled over
bumped against each other
with that accumulating
laughter
you love
and manufacture
so well in childhood
honest
from the heart
but with a look
of intrigue
yes
let go
and you are off
giggling and shaking
roaring uncontrollably
your song
and anyone not in it
looks sheepishly on
or cannot help
but be defined
as beaten parent
my father
waiting
'What's wrong'
he said
'They went to
Peasmarsh?'
then more overwhelming
we could have split
our sides
for good effect
burst buttons

we did laugh
till we cried
gasping
with gross sounds
like sobbing
from the back seat
of the Austin
up Kingston Hill
that Christmas
and my father waiting

and when Olaf
and Xenia
like figures
from two stories
the one the helpful Olaf
digging the hole
the other
from some Greek
tragedy
in her long black coat
for mourning
stood by your graveside
we traced our way
all eight of us
and mostly strangers
back down
Kingston Hill
to here
that cemetery
in Peasmarsh
where we put you
shaking first
with tears
then overcome
with laughter

***

If our childhood
was in black and white
those in Dickens
are in dingy greys
by Phiz
or Cruikshank

it's not surprising
in such rooms
they suffered
and the hell
of Bill Sykes
on the roof
or Fagin
before the gallows
became our bedtime
terrors

they lived in grey
so dingy
I had only found it
once
and lived in fear of it
an ill-lit
midnight hospital
away for the first time
unsleeping
as a child

our lives
moved on
like illustrations
waited for
at ends of chapters

not the coloured
frontispiece
or ill-fit
oranges and greens
of infant readers
but the big scenes
'He stumbled
as the ground gave way'
'Come back'
he cried
'I knew you'd come
to this'

and all our lives
I see
right now
just at this juncture
are seen
in captions
the person with the book
flicking through the pictures
'I'll be back'
not knowing
the story

***

Fifth Form at St Dominic's

You read the books
I could not read
even when I could
'Jock of the Bushveldt'
'The Insurgent Trail'
'Fifth Form at St Dominic's'

13

all foreign lands
and far too big
with too small print
and difficult
for me

you went there
every day
in grandpa's footsteps
I have his copper coasters
from the Hussars
his photo
in 'the Bushveldt'
cocked-hat
confident
unbuttoned

and for you
not quite the Balkans
but Biafra
and its fleeing people
you were helped
as much as helping
and learnt Africa
from a different
sort of book

my lot
if not 'St Dominic's'
was the posh
and braided blazer
surnames and Houses
sneaks and Colours

and with never
the slightest notion
you could think

until you told me
'How amazingly
you did
winning that scholarship'

my dismay
you could so credit me
with what I knew
was mere opportunity
my pleasure
that you said it
and my fierce desire
but knowing it would serve
no purpose
to set you right

* * *

'Book The First, Poverty' (Little Dorrit)

You never told
how Grandma Dolan
lived with not a bean
above the Rolls
her husband drove
as chauffeur

You never told
how our mother
made lampshades
just to keep afloat
telling our father
'Presents for friends'

You never told
how we as children
quite normally for those days
passed things on
your shoes
which always gave me blisters
my sister's coat
carved out of something else

Sergeant on National Service
perhaps you followed
King's Regulations
always keeping up a front
holding things together –
never letting the side down
as I do writing here

* * *

Keeping Up a Front

Keeping up a front –
how utterly impossible –
and the words
from our war days
or the weatherman
and without their space
effrontery *affront*

I think of clapboard
colours held up
by rough wood
at the back of it
quickly put together
by the sea

or at that other Front
not quite concealing
normal fear
and panic
getting ready
for The Show

or that other show
kept up
put-on
word-perfect
even in banter
which must go on

as you did
flawlessly
right through
to the curtain

***

The Prelude to 'Die Walkyrie'

Before the king died
or afterwards
I don't recall
but in the same hall
with the partitions
folded back
from classrooms
into a cinema
where Magwitch
among the gravestones
and poor Pip
frightened the life of us

and you collected prizes
and I hitched my trousers
and sang
'A Flaxen-headed Plough-boy'
and on important days
like the Coronation
flickering newsreels
were played
on the big screen
you boxed
and won
always the winner
so strange to say
at this point
but still
knocking down
Steerforth
and any bounder
still upright
always the elder brother
taking your place
in the long line
of fathers
while I
long since
had slunk away

***

Reading Women

Grandma read Dickens and Dumas
Little Nana told you 'Use
the Library
read
every week'

– I thought her love was cinema
but that brought comfort
in the raids
warmth in winter
somewhere to sit right through –

'History' she taught you
her family of Civil War
and Dublin
escape to 'Service'
and a great house

Lord Danckwerts'
who offered you
the Billiard Room
its full-sized table
while she got on

no wonder then
in the pub years later
baker and postman
dreaded
your game

as I learnt
after your funeral
somebody asking me
'Do *you* play pool?'
a glow of admiration
ready

'No'
I said
'But sometimes
and awfully'

***

Killer Instinct

Where did that come from
your killer instinct
always winner
my father good at
almost everything
was always a loser
too kind to win
until we scoffed
and then he tried
too much in love
with what was to be made
to think he'd make it
perfectly – but you
my brother
counting cars
or naming buses
swapping stamps
or shoving pennies
kicking at the gate
with other children
that much older
not just me
were always winner

what then
could such a person
have to do with death

my guess is
you had seen it
in the distance coming
like a sky-er
from the boundary
where all of us
saw only blinding sun

hands cupped and ready
pacing backwards
just not capable
of letting it drop

***

Class

I counted the goods trucks
always in eights
and how they bumped
and clattered to themselves
or ticked on
out of earshot
dozens hundreds
a schoolboy
in the playing-field
in 1948

while my brother
scored and tackled
all-rounder
captain
taken to one side
befriended
by the coach

three years later
my posh school
played them
once
at an age
which gave no danger
to our status

coming to the bumpy pitch
and endless outfield
where my brother
always top-scored

they put us
on the front lawn
perfect surface
proud to show
perhaps
they too had class
short boundaries
true bounce
and level wicket
we trounced them
to my shame

I bowled my heart out
just to show them
how far I had come
knew which side
I should have played on
and there was no way back

* * *

The Marshalsea

Poets both
me just about
still in short trousers
we joked of
Harold Skimpole
poet-scrounger
in *Bleak House*

joined our father
in his too true
echoing of Micawber
minding
pounds and pence

now you
never villainous
without the least capacity
to hurt anyone
in charge always
I see in the cancer ward
as 'The Father
of the Marshalsea'
Old Dorrit
dispensing little gifts
and kindness

years past
you lost
a Dickensian fortune
to an earthquake
in The East
and I heard
that plagued by
reams of papers
demanding this and that
you let them lie

it's not my story
I do not even know
how much of it
is fiction
I learnt no more of it
from you
than could be heard
in a small boat
on the river

watching as you rowed
engaged
in all that darkness
in getting us
ashore

* * *

Seafarer

So many ships abandoned
some not even holed
how easy it is for pirates
who clamber from the next
and then another
always afloat
or the steerfast captains
full-steam to the horizon
whether paradise island
or sea-monster hove to
beside them

> *Drake is in his hammock*
> *and a thousand miles away –*
> *Capten art tha sleepin there below*

or those so many
fast in slumber
who take their shilling
tot of rum
or climb the rigging
for the peace
of being look-out
knowing
they will be the first to see
whatever danger
beckons

Drake is in his hammock
and a thousand miles away –
Capten art tha sleepin there below

but the one
who walks the deck
dreaming of his father
and how he once
showed him the ropes
remembering
how he too
was all at sea
will hear a choir
of shipwrecked heroes
filling up his head
and words he memorized
for school prize-days –

Drake is in his hammock
and a thousand miles away –
Capten art tha sleepin there below

***

Elder Brother

I always saw myself
as Jack Point
Jester
and you as Colonel Fairfax
tenor
leading-man
although you had no voice
for singing

and near the end
you told me
you had slipped inside
our father's coffin
words from *The Yeomen*
'Is life a boon . . .'
unknown to me

such elder-brother action
taking it on yourself
doing it
whatever it is
by right
when I would never dream
of not asking

so when you died
like things from a school satchel
snatched
at the bus-stop
spilled out
not dreadful secrets
not scandals
just the tale
of being in charge
always

how could such pride
have let any of us
below the surface –
you were keeping up
the ones you cherished
holding above water
our good name

we long since
some with your teaching
had learnt well
how to swim

which made no difference
to watching
as you went under

***

The Yeoman of the Guard

'Food for fishes
only fitted
jester wishes
he was dead'

my first and only
part
and with a spring
and somersault

I was over the stage-edge
and on
to the green-room
door

a non-actor from the start
in a role
you never played
or wanted

you were still in costume
talking to 'The Headsman'
who would not believe
the show was over

***

The Bright Side

You never looked
on the bad side

I feel now
like a mudlark
from our father's
childhood
trying to find
something
for myself

hear the clatter
of the gulls
as if I rummaged
bin-liners
you had cast aside

the best side
of everyone
you looked for
as in silhouettes
of kings
and worthies
or those fifties
film-stars
who insisted on
being shot
from their
good side

meticulous
in this
so like our father
always on the ready

just in case
not worth looking
on the dark side

and when
the unexpected
visitor
did creep up
almost inaudibly
and then much louder
you looked ahead

* * *

Leeches

From tussock to tussock
the bad boys behind us
then their shouts diminished
and between each foothold
the oily water
grew more deep

we had talked of the marsh
filled it with serpents
grew sick and dizzy
at the thought of leeches
never ventured there
even for a dare

but we were hunted by hooligans
cornered
with no way back –
so each turn you took
as if it was a board-game
you could master

and your lead I followed
without stick
or light
in half-light
right through the marsh
until we made it

When the first quagmire
opened
decades later
you were drawn in slowly
so I've learned
held for months
without a sign of motion –

your partner found you
tried to piece together
what could possibly
have taken place –
and then the second

Years later
when you died
she found maps
of heroes
lists of footholds
smeared finger-prints

no sign of leeches

***

'Biggles Sees It Through'

My brother was Biggles
I was into Blyton's
Book of Naughty Children
identifying
with both their villainy
like mine
and their chastising

meanwhile he flew
to the Baltic
rescued even toffs
from the ice-flows
flew South
and East
moved on
to Stevenson
and Buchan

I graduated
fancying the heroine
with long legs
and scratched knees
from *The Island
of Adventure*

he never
really made it
safely back
from late in life
losing the rottweiler
he had called
'Bertie'

***

Opener

Statham to your Truman
Washbrook
to your Hutton
now you are picked
to partner Death
who will I choose

the obvious opener
guide to the underworld
Virgil
spoke Latin
and I never managed
that

so I'm alone descending
looking past
my shoulder
making sure
there's still
some light on
otherwise
I'll go no further

* * *

We

Your plural pronoun
always inclusive
in what you planned to do
and in anything you did without me
it was waiting there
for me soon to catch up

32

it took in Tennyson
and Hopkins T S Eliot
especially *Four Quartets*
Beethoven the great composers
you gave them in your plural
non-stop from the start

I offered later
William Carlos Williams
Haydn Ibsen
you were encouraging –
it made no difference
though you never took them up

I travelled in the singular
had no choice but left you
to National Service
The Queen's Bank
Old Coasters
and a multinational

you waited for my company
to come once more
and join you
faithful
to whatever once
we'd shared

but years back
I had happily abandoned
much of it
The Oval Stamford Bridge
The Albert Hall
The Last Night

though *that* you managed
perfectly

without its Pomp
and Circumstance
more Enigma Variations
a shared taste

* * *

Dylan Thomas

How you loved
Dylan Thomas
always the colour
of the words
the sentimentality
'alright'
and yes
especially
the fun
the golden
childhood
towering dead

I always thought
'Do Not Go Gentle'
after first impressions
more easily said
than done

When it came to it
your mind still wandered
a heron-priested shore
then went gently
into your own good night

* * *

'A Grief Ago' (Dylan Thomas)

From earliest childhood
you wept for trees
felled

Margaret grieving
'over golden-grove
un-leaving'
was your favourite poem

too many of those
to speak of
you made lists of them
the plangent note
and some believing

you too
were lost in boyhood
real life
was held
in high-flown language
taken beyond
our meanings

in the safe hands
of four movements
to a grand finale
Beethoven
with the final
answered shout
'O Freude'

yet you best loved
the loving fool
of Mozart

the bird-catcher
with home-spun
wisdom

rescued
for his song
so simple

as if there was
a place
where out of innocence
through music
dreams came true

* * *

The Wizard of Oz

What a group
in the waiting room
one of us
not too good
at standing upright
in this
one reduced
to silence
anxious
at the slightest roar
and one in sparkling shoes
dancing the three of us
towards death

I thought my brother
like the woodcutter
the Tin-man
impenetrable

if needing oil
ready
arm raised
in salutation
however bad
the situation
to defend
everything
he stood for

we were ushered in
one by one
and dreading
what we would find
little to be heard
his voice near-going
and so much to say
or best refrain from saying
keep close
to your chest

we left
knowing the wizard
had no more than
wheels and levers
safe only
while his curtain
kept him from sight
yet knowing that
took nothing
from the magic

lion grew courageous
scarecrow wiser
understood
the vulnerability
inevitable
in being straw

and he was Oz
and never Tin-man
had heart enough
for three of us

Dorothy
made it home
to wake up
alone

* * *

The Barracudas

My brother swimming
with barracudas
had his trunks
snipped neatly
as by tailors
deftly
as with singers
and the nearest
hottest fans

those waiting on the bank
were startled
by this naked man
speechless
rushing towards them
from untroubled water

* * *

Two Visits

Like a monarch
or a clown
or an MP
choosing to pause
and swap words
as if the consultant
yet you were the patient

As if Jesus on the way
to Emmaus
or Holman Hunt's
'Light of the World'
come back
out of our childhood picture
yet I was the visitor
leaving

looking towards
the half-light
the low ceiling
and you there
on the sofa
looking up
watching my going

the wave back
the lifted hand
and that was that

***

Phone

The bad line
cleared
each gap
and struggle
loss of voice
poor hearing
was our own

we shared
a bad joke
forced laughter

the silence
following
was powerless
against your feeble
punch-line

***

The Usual

Meeting you
a little mischief
always tinged
our greeting

as if the door
was already open
and a lock-in waited
there for the choosing

evening stretching
like that bay
in Africa
nothing on tomorrow

even there
in the bedside chair
with you masked
as if for pollen

and wired up
for the present
beside the blank
of the bed

you took up
my greeting
as if our next move
would be out

then shyness
made a language
we must master
quickly

and we did
until my thumb lifted
your thumb
answered

and our eyes
settled on
a new
expression

closer
than looking up
to ask
'The usual'

knowing
the answer

Postcards from Germany

You may have experienced travelling some distance to see a picture and finding that it is on loan, in conservation, just not currently on display. On one such occasion I was offered, in recompense, a postcard. These poems are postcards for those who may not have the opportunity to see the originals.

1

Rhine Cruise

Like Dixieland
thrown overboard
by the gold and silver
bucketful
onto the flat Mississippi
the Edwardian bandstand
of the boat
ships song
from nightingale and thrush
at each sharp turn of river
if only those aboard
could hear them

Bonn

The green parakeet
escaped
to the great elm
above the tomb
of Clara Schumann
cannot make it back
to the wall
of Macke's attic
and complete
the *Paradise*
he left unfinished there
with Marc

Mainz

Helmetted in stone
beside their gods
they stand guard
over the ribs
of a Rhine barge
hauled up
from the centuries'
latest low

the Opel Astra
which rose
like Aphrodite
from the water
exposing its driver
still safely belted
went for scrap

Stuttgart

When the lightning
fizzed straight through
the glass dome
of Karstadt
and landed
between a Steiff zebra
and a horse
at that very moment
being groomed
in plastic

thirty miles north
the lights flickered
at Marbach
revealing
to a manuscripteuse
a comma in Schiller
left hitherto unobserved
or perhaps
a thunderfly
from the nearby barley

Trier

The birch-bark card
written from Hadrian's Wall
demanding wine
to bring the Mosel's
flowery Riesling
up the brackish Tyne
was never posted

but charabancs
of Geordies
cradle the incense
of Glühwein
at each Christmas Fair

Koblenz

Turner stood and saw
the boring Ehrenbreitstein
catch fire
with light

you may have to stand
all day
on Platform 44
and still not hear
from the abandoned barracks
'Lights Out'

2

Seebüll

Colours run
from hollyhock
and dahlia
into the near sea's
breakers

moonlight
takes to water
as currents
of marigold
and vetch

choose
a vase
to carry off
the blooms
of water

or choose a boat
to bring you
sea
marbled
with anemone

Bremen

So many slender bricks
could bear the weight
of longing
or bear the burden
of security
with no outward sign
of stress

a row of silver birches
could be spaced apart
to make a hedge
to keep a prince out
or make pillars
to let sunlight
fall through

if you are used to
a flat landscape
perhaps you hold
and carry with you
all you need
to fill the space
of sky

The Friesian Islands

The sea cannot achieve
what sand does
taking our weight
leaving our shapes
in its lap
till the wind lifts up
grain after grain
our shadows
and nobody can know
who lay between
the tufts of eel grass
in the pooled light
of midday

Hanover

The Hungarian musician
clothed their evening
in such strange fabrics
they were relieved
to strip off
and fall into each other
in bed

next day
the cleaner's knock
was left unnoticed
you might have seen them
board the Warsaw train

she was covered in flowers
embroidered white and red
he had the smile
of a high note
on a violin

Heidelberg

You could expect
to find in the castle sandstone
two lovers'
moon-like faces
as in a childhood puzzle-picture

or hope to see their hands
held tightly
in the unknown alphabet
of wet tiles

or catch a glimpse
of winter coats
in chimney smoke

they left their prints
apart
and then together
in snow

Neustadt an der Weinstrasse

Cowparsley and hogweed
left space enough
for them to lie
where the goods-yard wall
gave back sunshine
as stored shade

they moved
no more than trains
at platforms
seem to move
as others
draw away

that afternoon
still as scarecrows
out of place
beside the vineyards
leaves in their hair
they had paused
at the forest edge
and wondered
at the sunlight
where deer now graze

3

Krefeld Textile Museum

If you tried to follow
every line of stitches
you would never leave
the frame

you could try to circle
each momentary light
of a sequin
and never see yourself

but if you slide your finger
up a needle's sides
and stitch

you can perch
like Ariel
in its eye

Cologne Wallraf-Richartz Museum

Carry on walking
past the end
of Platform 1
and you will pass
restored twin towers

beside a leader
on a great
green horse
turn right

and you will hear
that an old man
dying of laughter
is expected
at any moment

Kaiserslautern Pfalz Museum

They've moved the picture
of the woman stitching

divorced the portrait
of a painter's wife

outside the gallery
God's hand

is still spread out
above the shoppers

throttled back
to land at Ramstein

Worpswede Artists' Colony

Sat on chairs
they cannot fall

like jugs
made out of worsted
they could not break

the baby brought
with last month's post
like a new-risen loaf
on the table-cloth
never kicks up a fuss

chill draughts halt
at this tapestry
where a woman
bare-breasted
holds up a sunflower
to light the room

Darmstadt Jugendstil Quarter

Going up the steps
to Hollywood
under a Lohengrin
starry sky
how can you find
a way in

the gilded dragonflies
cannot take off
a glass fountain chokes
on bubbles of silver
the mosaic beds of flowers
cry out for decay

Berlin National Gallery

Past the wine tasters
past the lost knights
the granite fountain
for Charlottenburg
past the stately picnics
the old towns
the older generals
in plumes and fur
people disappear

and you may hear
the measurement
of silences
the chronometers
of sheer drops
the weighing up
of darkness
tumbling
out of sky

if you turn
your back

Frankfurt am Main Museums

Each plane tree
designed
by Yves Tanguy
you can look for
Greta Garbo
and find
Cranach's
Audrey Hepburn
wearing nothing
but a hat

4

Essen

Glens and crags
and cumulus of rhododendron
to grace Northumberland
issued from the mouth
of Armstrong's
sixteen-inch naval gun

here a wedding-cake villa
complete with romantic gardens
for the love of nature
dropped from Krupp's
Big Bertha

each retreat
affords
the same view

The Mosel Magnate

Plunge in his pool
and swim to Mexico
and back
on the Gulf Stream
he brought home for nothing
in the sixties

drink his wine
stored in sarcophagi
which Romans would have envied
their dead
coming up
like the best Bordeaux

his Venus de Milo
with broken arms
on the fifth of six terraces
has crayoned nipples

Völklingen

Why don't they let
those three boys
and two girls
one a tomboy
with a dog
unpick the rusted padlock
to the great barred gates
and find the treasure map
of the abandoned
iron works

the teacher explains
how many rivets
made each boiler
how much coal
went up in smoke
how much rust
was sanded off
to make
this monument
to industrial decay
but could not let them in

Mülheim an der Ruhr

Four pots of de-caf
a sans souci of sugar
the thoughtfulness
of fork through cake
they make
a colour-card
in pale delphinium
primrose and magenta
and a little way ahead
and taller
champagne

they pluck umbrellas
from the empty hatstand
like choosing gladioli
for a grave
and vanish
into rain

Bad Nauheim

The Casino burnt down
long before Dostoevsky
had the chance
to lose there

heart patients patrol
its gardens
passing their time
in winter

stretch out a hand
with a crumb of hope
for a bird to land
and ring their finger

5

Ludwigshafen

A cube
from a kindergarten
big enough
to climb right in
and find
a station
long enough
to arrive
without a train
and meet
a perfect stranger
who asks
tenderly
was last night
just as good for you

Wiesbaden

The Russian church
is small enough
for a Russian doll
inside another doll
with a round green face
and purple cheekbones
inside another doll
face large enough
to be your mother's
seen from her lap
inside another doll
a Russian church
with onion domes
peeled to the core
a black line
making a lintel
and no door

Mannheim

Each year
the Lewis chessmen
glide through
the grid plan streets
in hope to find
the entrance
where one February
each faceless pawn
grew features
and played
the fool's day king

Oldenburg

The tailored houses
lean back
flat
as illustrations
wait
for a child's hand
to lift them
so a Pied Piper
from behind that fountain
can marvel at
the lack of rats

Halle

the jowelled
organist
went
and lit up London

leaving behind
two dots
like a lost cufflink
on the mantlepiece
of 'a'

choirs
of cumulus nimbus
raise the roof

6

Munich

Men turn to fisticuffs
in full evening dress
over the nearest slot
in the empty
theatre car park

overhead
the circus saints
cling on to painted marble
and little boys
show off their bums

here the Alps extend
their invitation
to the radiant blue
empty as a postcard
for you to write

Kiel

An honour-guard
of Jahn's gymnasts
in rompers
(1903)
guarantee
safe-passage
for the golden bride
stepped down
from a time-piece

flocks
of red-sailed Mirrors
in the harbour
bulge
with promise
steel masts
wink back

Hamburg

You could travel
in *MV Hamlet*'s belly
right up the Elbe
tempted by sirens
by a brass-band in a suitcase
by a ship's melancholy horn
your hands
trying to wipe off
the stench of diesel
your ears trying to silence
the noise of elephant seals
mating all night
under your bunk

and when you touched land
you could find
a bar
with an Irish uncle
teaching customers
how pool billiards
is not a matter of luck

Tübingen

The new year
ushers in the sixties

a solitary police car
splutters into the square

a pair of elderly officers
descend and wait

an ornate clock sets off
a hundred church bells

the car describes
a circle

leaves
an empty square

Karlsruhe

Girls bring
bouquets
of grasses
to be named

a woman
with a pushchair
growing
from her fingers

trots
upright as a lipizaner
past two green
policemen

who consult
a gardener
about the laws
of light and shade

Aschaffenburg

Hold on
the wind is blowing
and your last chance
to write

if you are not careful
the whole thing
will be smudged
with rain

they open locks here
where in darkness
you could perform a miracle
and no one would know

be patient
the castle clock
will half-complete
its winter carillon

tombs
in the Stiftskirche
will nearly prove
death right

the divided river
will wander on
soon taken
in another's arms

and lost
only to sight

The Postmaster

He is leaning
in a blue jacket
his head towards the window
not looking
at anything there

he has a pencil
books beside him
maps and papers
and whatever secret
they revealed
he has already moved
into his head

he will deliver
latitude
and angle
how long it takes
to get there
and where

look long
and close enough
you may make it
right here

Acknowledgements

I would like to thank the editors of the following journals in which poems from this collection have previously appeared, often under different titles and in different versions: *The Eildon Tree, Fiddlehead* (Canada), *Frogmore Papers, The Interpreter's House, Other Poetry, Poetry Salzburg Review, Stand.*

The likely personal debts behind a sequence such as 'Poems for Alan' will be self-evident: here I acknowledge, with heartfelt thanks, the support of Rhona Stylianou and Stephen Graham. A collection of poems by my brother is in preparation. 'Postcards from Germany' I have dedicated to my German friends – and friends in Germany – over many years, in gratitude for the generosity of their friendship. Many of the postcards could have carried specific dedications but my chosen format does not allow that – Germany is the poems' subject, not friendship. Two 'Postcards', however, do require particular dedications which I can give here: 'Karlsruhe' is dedicated 'to Liz Shipley', 'Stuttgart' 'to Ulrike Böhmer-Dinç'. In many cases friendship has overlapped with and grown from professional contacts. I would, therefore like to add a formal acknowledgement of the creative support given over the years by repeated invitations to read and discuss my work, from Dr Walter Bachem, Dr Gordon Collier, Jack Debney, Prof. Dr Lothar Fietz, Prof. Dr Michael Gassenmeier, Prof. Dr Martin Kuester, Prof. Dr Norbert Platz, Prof. Dr Manfred Pfister, Prof. Dr Bernhard Reitz, Prof. Dr Karen Vogt and Dr Dieter Wessels. None of these people, of course, has the least responsibility for the views and nature of the poems.

My thanks to Flambard once again for their professional care and their support; to Carol Rumens for her clear-eyed reading of the poems, as well as her creative friendship; to Edward Martin for his scrupulous, sensitive sharing of the texts; to Neil Hairsine for the subtlety of his insights; to Gordon and Wilma Meade for once again sustaining my writing through close criticism and support; and to Trude and Milena who understand poetry better than I do.

The nature of such a collection means that the old watchword of authors applies here with especial force – these poems could not have been made without the help of others: whatever the poems' shortcomings, they are my own.

Newcastle upon Tyne/Kirchheimbolanden, January 2009